3 Days in Berlin Travel Guide

Welcome to the ultimate **travel guide to Berlin**! This guide is designed to help you make the most of your visit to this vibrant and fascinating city. Whether you're a first-time visitor or a seasoned traveler, Berlin has something for everyone, from historic landmarks and world-class museums to trendy neighborhoods and a thriving food and drink scene.

In this guide, you'll find everything you need to plan your perfect trip, including detailed information on the city's history, culture, and geography, practical information on getting around and staying safe, and insider tips on the best places to eat, drink, and explore.

We've also included suggested itineraries for **one-day to five-day** trips, so you can experience the highlights of the city and its surrounding areas at your own pace.

So let's dive in and discover everything that Berlin has to offer!

Contents

Shopping in Berlin- 32

Nightlife in Berlin- 35

Day Trips from Berlin- 38

A 3-Day Travel Itinerary for First Timers -47

One-Day Itinerary: Highlights of Berlin- 76

Two-Day Itinerary:Historic Berlin &Trendy Neighborhoods-78

Four-Day Itinerary: Day Trips from Berlin- 81

Five-Day Itinerary: Berlin and Beyond- 82

Practical Information for Visiting Berlin- 83

Thank You!

Copyright Notice

Introduction to Berlin

Berlin, the capital city of Germany, is a vibrant and dynamic metropolis that seamlessly blends rich history with modern innovation. This bustling city has a fascinating past that can be seen in its stunning architecture, museums, and monuments, as well as a thriving art and music scene. With a diverse population of over 3.5 million people, Berlin is a melting pot of cultures, languages, and ideas. Whether you're interested in history, culture, nightlife, or simply exploring a new city, Berlin has something to offer everyone.

Overview of Berlin's history, culture, and geography

Berlin has a rich and complex history that has shaped its culture and geography in unique ways. Originally a small trading post on the River Spree, Berlin grew to become the capital of Prussia in the 18th century and the capital of Germany in the 19th century. Throughout the 20th century, Berlin played a pivotal role in some of the world's most significant historical events, including World War II and the Cold War. Today, Berlin is known for its stunning architecture, world-class museums and galleries, thriving art and music scene, and diverse culinary offerings. Located in the eastern part of Germany, Berlin is surrounded by forests, lakes, and parks, providing ample opportunities for outdoor recreation.

The History of Berlin

Berlin, the capital of Germany, has a rich and complex history that spans more than eight centuries. Throughout this time, the city has undergone significant changes, from being a small trading town to becoming one of the most important cultural and political centers in Europe.

One of the most significant events in the history of Berlin was the division of the city after World War II. At the end of the war, Germany was divided into four occupation zones, controlled by the United States, Great Britain, France, and the

Soviet Union. Berlin, as the capital of Germany, was also divided into four sectors, with each of the Allied powers controlling one sector. The Soviet Union, which had suffered the most losses during the war, took the eastern part of the city, while the other three powers took the western part.

The division of the city was not intended to be permanent, but as the Cold War intensified, the relationship between the Soviet Union and the Western powers deteriorated, and the division became more entrenched. In 1961, the East German government, with the support of the Soviet Union, built a wall around West Berlin, cutting off the city from the rest of East Germany and the Soviet-controlled territories. The wall became a symbol of the Cold War and the division of Europe, and its fall in 1989 marked a significant moment in the history of Berlin and the world.

The reunification of Germany in 1990 brought significant changes to Berlin, as the city became the capital of a united Germany. The process of reunification was not without challenges, as the economic and social differences between the former East and West Germany were significant. However, over the past three decades, Berlin has become a thriving and cosmopolitan city, known for its vibrant culture, history, and innovation.

The history of Berlin is closely intertwined with the history of Russia, as the Soviet Union played a significant role in the city's development and division. After the war, the Soviet Union rebuilt and modernized the eastern part of the city, creating a socialist state with a planned economy and a strong emphasis on industry and infrastructure. The Soviet Union also established a strong political presence in the city, with its embassy and other institutions located in the heart of East Berlin.

The relationship between the Soviet Union and East Germany was complex, with tensions and disagreements arising from time to time. However, the Soviet Union remained a close ally and supporter of East Germany until the end of the Cold War. After the fall of the Berlin Wall, the Soviet Union withdrew its troops from Germany, and its influence in the city waned.

Today, Berlin is a thriving and diverse city that embraces its complex history and the different cultures that have contributed to its development. The city is home to numerous museums, galleries, and monuments that tell the story of its past, including the Berlin Wall Memorial, the Brandenburg Gate, and the Reichstag Building. The city's vibrant cultural scene, with its music, art, and theater, reflects the diversity of its inhabitants and the different influences that have shaped the city over time.

In conclusion, the history of Berlin is a complex and fascinating story that reflects the challenges and opportunities of the past century. From its division during the Cold War to its reunification and its emergence as a thriving cultural and political center, Berlin has undergone significant changes that have shaped its identity and character. Today, Berlin is a city that celebrates its history while looking to the future, a place of diversity, innovation, and creativity that continues to inspire and captivate visitors from around the world.

Important facts and figures about the city

- Berlin is the largest city in Germany and the second most populous city in the European Union after London.
- The city covers an area of 891.8 square kilometers (344.3 square miles).
- Berlin is divided into 12 boroughs, each with its own unique character and attractions.
- The population of Berlin is over 3.5 million people, with a diverse mix of nationalities and cultures.
- Berlin is a major center for politics, culture, science, and media, with numerous universities, research institutions, and media companies based in the city.

- Berlin has a rich cultural heritage, with world-famous museums and galleries, as well as a thriving contemporary art and music scene.
- Berlin has a temperate climate, with mild summers and cold winters. Average temperatures in summer range from 18 to 23°C (64 to 73°F), while average temperatures in winter range from -2 to 4°C (28 to 39°F).
- Berlin is well-connected to the rest of Germany and Europe, with two international airports, several train stations, and an extensive public transportation system.
- The currency used in Berlin is the Euro (EUR).
- Berlin is a relatively affordable city compared to other major European capitals, with a wide range of accommodation options and dining choices to suit all budgets.

Getting to and around Berlin

Getting to Berlin: Berlin is well-connected to the rest of Germany and Europe, with two international airports, several train stations, and highways leading into the city.

By Plane:

Berlin has two airports: Tegel Airport (TXL) and Schönefeld Airport (SXF). In 2020, Berlin opened its new airport, Berlin Brandenburg Airport (BER). Visitors can fly to Berlin from many major cities around the world, with airlines such as Lufthansa, British Airways, and Ryanair offering direct flights. Prices vary depending on the airline, route, and time of year. Visitors can book flights online through airline websites or through travel booking sites such as Expedia or Kayak.

By Train:

has several train stations, with the main one being Berlin Hauptbahnhof. Visitors can travel to Berlin by train from many cities in Germany and throughout Europe, with Deutsche Bahn being the main railway company. Train fares vary depending on the route and time of day, with prices generally being lower if booked in advance. Visitors can book train tickets online through the Deutsche Bahn website.

By Car:

Visitors can drive to Berlin on Germany's extensive network of highways. Berlin is located at the intersection of several major highways, including the A2, A9, and A10. Visitors can rent cars from major rental companies such as Sixt, Europcar, and Avis.

Getting Around Berlin:

Berlin has an extensive public transportation system, including buses, trams, trains, and a subway system called the U-Bahn. The city is also known for its bike-friendly streets, with bike lanes throughout the city and bike rental stations available for visitors.

By Public Transportation: Visitors can purchase tickets for public transportation at ticket vending machines located in most stations or through the BVG app. Single tickets cost €2.90 and are valid for up to 2 hours of travel within the city. Visitors can also purchase day tickets, which cost €8.60 and allow for unlimited travel within the city for a full day. More information on public transportation in Berlin can be found on the BVG website.

By Bike: Visitors can rent bikes through companies such as Nextbike, Mobike, and Lime. Prices vary depending on the company, with some offering hourly rentals and others offering daily or weekly rentals. Visitors can find bike rental stations throughout the city, with many located near major tourist attractions. More information on bike rentals in Berlin can be found on the Berlin.de website.

By Taxi: Taxis are widely available in Berlin, with fares starting at €3.90 and increasing based on distance traveled and time of day. Visitors can hail a taxi on the street or through ride-sharing apps such as Uber or Lyft.

Overall, Berlin has a variety of transportation options to suit all needs and budgets, making it easy for visitors to get around the city and explore all that it has to offer.

#1: **Berlin is an enormous city**. It's the largest capital in Europe, overcoming cities like London or Paris, even if it's much less densely populated. So, as much as we like improvising while we're discovering new cities, designing a good day plan for every day is critical. If you don't do this, you take the risk of wandering around and walking the city for hours without finding anything particularly interesting.

#2: Considering the size of the city, the smart **use of public transport will be absolutely essential** for your visit. Get a "Berlin Welcome Card," which costs 19€ but will give you unlimited transport (subway, bus, and tram) for your entire stay. This card also provides 50% discounts at some museums and attractions.

#3: **Try to visit Berlin during the summer**. The city is freezing during winter, autumn, and sometimes even spring. On summer, the weather is simply perfect, and the whole town changes for the better: Berliners seem to be much happier, and everyone is out on the streets.

#4: **Berlin offers a lot of free walking tours** that guide you through the city's most famous monuments and last about 5 hours. They are an excellent option for getting a first glimpse of the city, especially because all of the rich histories that are behind every building.

#5: If you're interested in dining at a restaurant at some point, consider that a **10% of the total tip for the waiter is what's considered standard**. And you have to ask the waiter to include it on the ticket; it's considered a rude behavior to only leave the money on the table while you leave, just the way it's done in many other countries.

#6: **Berlin doesn't have one single city center**: it has many different parts along its massive extension that can each be considered as a *center*. But on this guide, we will refer mostly to the **Mitte** neighborhood as the heart of Berlin since it's where most of the most famous and emblematic buildings and monuments are.

Depending on which Airport you arrive at, you have different options for getting to the center of the city (Mitte).

Berlin Tegel Airport (TXL)

Berlin Schönefeld Airport (SFX)

Tegel Airport is only 8 km away from the center of Berlin. If you arrive here, you have to take a bus to go to the heart of the city (there are no trains from Tegel).

TXL is the most famous bus line, which can take you straight to Alexanderplatz. If you need to go to the Western side of Berlin, take the **109** or the **X9 bus lines**. Finally, if you are staying at the North part of the city, which would be near Tegel Airport itself, take the 128 bus line.

A taxi to the center of Berlin from Tegel Airport takes about **20 minutes** and **costs 20€-25€.**

If you arrive at **Schönefeld**, then the situation is a little bit more complicated than arriving at Tegel, but not difficult either. If you need to get to the East or Northeast of the city, take the **S9 metropolitan train**. If you need to get to Southern Berlin, take the **SFX Airport Express Bus**. Finally, if you need to go to the Alexanderplatz area, the best option is the **RE7** or **RB14 trains**.

After 11 PM, transport from Schönefeld Airport to the city is more difficult because most public transports are not working. However, in this situation, you still have 2 options. The first one is to take the night bus N7, and the second one is to simply take a taxi, which would cost around 40 € to the center of Berlin.

Top Attractions in Berlin

Berlin is a city with a rich cultural heritage, stunning architecture, and a vibrant arts scene. From world-famous museums and galleries to historical monuments and landmarks, Berlin has something to offer everyone. Here are some of the top attractions that you won't want to miss during your visit to Berlin.

Brandenburg Gate

One of the most iconic landmarks in Berlin, the Brandenburg Gate is a must-see attraction for any visitor to the city. Located in the heart of Berlin, the Brandenburg Gate is a neoclassical triumphal arch that dates back to the 18th century. It has become a symbol of Berlin and Germany's tumultuous history, serving as the site of many significant historical events over the years.

History: The Brandenburg Gate was designed by Carl Gotthard Langhans and was completed in 1791. It was commissioned by King Frederick William II of Prussia as a symbol of peace and prosperity. Over the years, the Brandenburg Gate has witnessed many significant historical events, including the rise of the Nazis, World War II, and the fall of the Berlin Wall.

Interesting facts:

- The Brandenburg Gate is one of the few remaining structures from the original Berlin Wall.

- The statue on top of the Brandenburg Gate is called the Quadriga and depicts a chariot drawn by four horses.

- The Brandenburg Gate was heavily damaged during World War II and underwent extensive restoration in the 2000s.

Visiting: The Brandenburg Gate is open 24 hours a day, and there is no admission fee to see it. Visitors can take a stroll through the gate or take a guided tour to learn more about its history and significance. There are also several nearby attractions worth visiting, including the Reichstag Building and the Holocaust Memorial. More information on visiting the Brandenburg Gate can be found on the Berlin.de website.

Berlin Wall

The Berlin Wall is one of the most famous landmarks in Berlin, serving as a powerful symbol of the city's divided past. The Wall was built in 1961 by the Communist government of East Germany to prevent citizens from escaping to the West. It stood for nearly three decades until it was finally torn down in 1989, signaling the end of the Cold War and the reunification of Germany.

History:

The Berlin Wall was erected overnight on August 13, 1961, dividing the city of Berlin into East and West. The Wall was made of concrete and barbed wire and was heavily guarded by armed soldiers. Over the years, many people attempted to escape over or under the Wall, often at great personal risk. The fall of the Wall on November 9, 1989, marked a significant turning point in German history and led to the reunification of East and West Germany.

Interesting facts:

- The Berlin Wall was not just one wall, but a complex system of walls, fences, and watchtowers that ran through the city.
- Over 5,000 people successfully escaped from East Berlin to West Berlin during the years of the Wall's existence.
- Parts of the Wall have been preserved and can be seen in various locations around Berlin, including the East Side Gallery and the Berlin Wall Memorial.

Visiting:

Visitors to Berlin can see the remains of the Berlin Wall at several locations throughout the city. The most famous section is the East Side Gallery, a 1.3-kilometer stretch of the Wall that has been transformed into an outdoor gallery featuring murals and artwork from around the world. Other notable locations include the Berlin Wall Memorial, which offers a comprehensive look at the history of the Wall, and Checkpoint Charlie, a former border crossing that has been turned into a museum. More information on visiting the Berlin Wall can be found on the Visit Berlin website.

Checkpoint Charlie

Checkpoint Charlie is a former border crossing point that served as the gateway between East and West Berlin during the Cold War. It was the most famous border crossing point, and its name comes from the NATO phonetic alphabet: "Charlie" stood for "C", which was the third letter in the alphabet, representing the third checkpoint on the Berlin Wall.

History:

Checkpoint Charlie was established in 1961 after the construction of the Berlin Wall, and it became the primary crossing point for Allied forces, diplomats, and foreigners traveling between East and West Berlin. The checkpoint was a tense and heavily guarded area, with American and Soviet tanks facing off against each other in a standoff that became known as the "Tank Standoff at Checkpoint Charlie."

Interesting facts:

- Checkpoint Charlie was the site of several famous Cold War events, including the escape of East German soldier Conrad Schumann over the barbed wire fence in 1961.
- The checkpoint was also the site of several spy exchanges between the United States and the Soviet Union.
- After the fall of the Berlin Wall in 1989, Checkpoint Charlie became a popular tourist attraction, with a replica of the original checkpoint and guardhouse erected on the site.

Visiting:

Visitors to Berlin can visit Checkpoint Charlie to learn more about its history and significance during the Cold War. There is a museum on the site that features exhibits on the Berlin Wall, the history of Checkpoint Charlie, and the various attempts to escape from East Berlin. Visitors can also take photos with actors dressed as American and Soviet soldiers, as well as visit nearby shops selling Cold War memorabilia. More information on visiting Checkpoint Charlie can be found on the Visit Berlin website and at www.mauermuseum.de.

Museum Island

Museum Island is a unique cultural complex located in the heart of Berlin. It is a UNESCO World Heritage site and is home to some of the most important museums and galleries in the world, showcasing a vast array of artwork, artifacts, and historical objects.

History:

Museum Island was founded in the 19th century, during the reign of King Frederick William IV of Prussia. The complex was designed to house the collections of the Prussian Royal Family and included five museums: the Altes Museum, the Neues Museum, the Alte Nationalgalerie, the Bode Museum, and the Pergamon Museum. Over the years, the collections grew, and the museums underwent extensive renovation and expansion projects to accommodate them.

Interesting facts:

- The Pergamon Museum is home to one of the world's most famous archaeological exhibits: the Pergamon Altar, a massive Hellenistic monument that dates back to the 2nd century BC.

- The Neues Museum houses the famous bust of Queen Nefertiti, one of the most well-known works of ancient Egyptian art.

- Museum Island has been under extensive renovation and restoration work in recent years, with many of the museums reopening to the public in the past decade.

Visiting:

Visitors to Berlin can purchase a ticket to visit all five museums on Museum Island, or they can purchase tickets for individual museums. The museums are open daily, and there are guided tours available for those who want to learn more about the collections. Visitors should be prepared for crowds, especially during peak tourist season, and should plan to spend several hours exploring the museums. More information on visiting Museum Island can be found on the **Museum Island Berlin** website: www.smb.museum/en/museums-institutions/museum-island-berlin/home.html.

Reichstag Building

The **Reichstag Building** is one of the most iconic landmarks in Berlin and is the home of the German parliament, known as the Bundestag. The building is located in the heart of Berlin and is renowned for its unique architectural design and fascinating history.

History:

The Reichstag Building was first opened in 1894 as the home of the German parliament. It has a long and complicated history, including being set on fire in 1933, bombed during World War II, and left in ruins during the Cold War. After the reunification of Germany, the Reichstag Building underwent an extensive renovation and restoration project, which included the addition of a new glass dome designed by British architect Sir Norman Foster.

Interesting facts:

- The Reichstag Building's glass dome is one of its most popular attractions and offers stunning views of the city.

- The Reichstag Building has witnessed many significant historical events, including the rise of the Nazi party, World War II, and the reunification of Germany.

- The building is surrounded by several other significant landmarks, including the Brandenburg Gate and the Holocaust Memorial.

Visiting:

Visitors to Berlin can take a guided tour of the Reichstag Building, which includes a visit to the glass dome and a tour of the parliamentary chamber. Admission to the Reichstag Building is free, but visitors must register in advance through the Bundestag website. Visitors should be aware that security measures are in place at the building, and they may need to go through a security check before entering. More information on visiting the Reichstag Building can be found on the **Bundestag** website: www.bundestag.de/en/visittheBundestag.

Berliner Dom

The **Berliner Dom** is a stunning cathedral located on Museum Island in the heart of Berlin. It is one of the most significant landmarks in the city and is renowned for its impressive architecture and rich history.

History:

The Berliner Dom was built in the early 20th century and served as the court church of the Prussian royal family. It was heavily damaged during World War II and underwent extensive restoration work in the 1970s and 1980s. Today, the Berliner Dom is open to the public and is a popular destination for tourists and locals alike.

Interesting facts:

- The Berliner Dom is home to the largest pipe organ in Germany, with over 7,000 pipes.

- The cathedral's dome is over 98 meters high, offering stunning views of the surrounding city.

- The Berliner Dom is home to several notable works of art, including a marble altar by Friedrich Drake and a bronze sculpture by Otto Lessing.

Visiting:

Visitors to Berlin can take a guided tour of the Berliner Dom, which includes a visit to the cathedral's interior, as well as access to the dome for panoramic views of the city. Admission to the Berliner Dom is required, and tickets can be purchased on-site or in advance through the Berliner Dom website. Visitors should be aware that the Berliner Dom is a functioning church, and they may need to adjust their visit to accommodate services or events. More information on visiting the Berliner Dom can be found on the **Berliner Dom** website: www.berlinerdom.de/en/.

Pergamon Museum

The **Pergamon Museum** is one of the most famous museums in Berlin and is renowned for its extensive collection of ancient artifacts and architecture. The museum is located on Museum Island and is home to several significant exhibits, including the famous Pergamon Altar.

History:

The Pergamon Museum was founded in the early 20th century and is named after its most famous exhibit, the Pergamon Altar. The museum underwent extensive renovation and expansion work in the 2000s and is now one of the largest and most visited museums in Germany.

Interesting facts:

- The Pergamon Museum is home to several ancient structures, including the Ishtar Gate of Babylon and the Market Gate of Miletus.

- The museum's most famous exhibit, the Pergamon Altar, is a massive Hellenistic monument that dates back to the 2nd century BC.

- The Pergamon Museum is part of the Berlin State Museums group, which includes several other museums and galleries on Museum Island and throughout the city.

Visiting:

Visitors to Berlin can purchase a ticket to visit the Pergamon Museum, as well as the other museums on Museum Island, or they can purchase tickets for individual museums. Admission to the Pergamon Museum is €19 for adults and is free for children under the age of 18. Visitors can also purchase a Berlin WelcomeCard, which offers discounts on admission to museums and other attractions throughout the city. More information on visiting the Pergamon Museum can be found on the **Pergamon Museum** website: www.smb.museum/en/museums-institutions/pergamonmuseum/home.html.

Berlin Zoo

The **Berlin Zoo** is one of the oldest and most famous zoos in the world, located in the heart of Berlin. It is home to over 20,000 animals from around the world and offers a unique and exciting experience for visitors of all ages.

History: The Berlin Zoo was founded in the mid-19th century and has a long and storied history. It was heavily damaged during World War II and underwent extensive renovation work in the 1950s and 1960s. Today, the Berlin Zoo is one of the most visited tourist attractions in the city and is renowned for its conservation efforts and commitment to animal welfare.

Interesting facts:

- The Berlin Zoo is home to over 1,500 species of animals, including giant pandas, elephants, and polar bears.

- The zoo has several notable exhibits, including the nocturnal animal house, the insectarium, and the aquarium.

- The Berlin Zoo is also home to the Tierpark Berlin, a large outdoor wildlife park located on the outskirts of the city.

Visiting: Visitors to Berlin can purchase tickets to the Berlin Zoo online or on-site. Ticket prices vary depending on the time of year and the type of ticket purchased. Visitors should plan to spend several hours at the zoo to see all of the exhibits and animals. The zoo also offers guided tours and special events throughout the year. More information on visiting the Berlin Zoo can be found on the **Berlin Zoo** website: www.zoo-berlin.de/en.

East Side Gallery

The **East Side Gallery** is a unique open-air art gallery located on the former site of the Berlin Wall. It is the largest remaining section of the Berlin Wall, and it is home to over 100 murals and works of street art.

History:

The East Side Gallery was created shortly after the fall of the Berlin Wall in 1989 as a way to commemorate the peaceful revolution and to celebrate the reunification of Germany. It features murals and paintings by artists from around the world and has become one of the most popular tourist attractions in Berlin.

Interesting facts:

- The East Side Gallery is home to several famous works of street art, including the "My God, Help Me to Survive This Deadly Love" mural, also known as the "Fraternal Kiss."

- The gallery is over a kilometer long, making it the longest open-air gallery in the world.

- The East Side Gallery has been the subject of several preservation efforts, including restoration work on the murals and efforts to protect the gallery from development.

Visiting:

Visitors to Berlin can visit the East Side Gallery for free and can walk along the length of the wall to see the various murals and works of art. The gallery is located near several other notable landmarks, including the Oberbaum Bridge and the Berlin Wall Memorial. Visitors should be aware that the East Side Gallery can be crowded, especially during peak tourist season. More information on visiting the East Side Gallery can be found on the **East Side Gallery** website: www.eastsidegallery-berlin.de.

Neighborhoods of Berlin

Berlin is a diverse and multicultural city with many distinct neighborhoods to explore. Each neighborhood has its own unique character and charm, from the historic streets of Mitte to the trendy cafes of Friedrichshain. Here are a few of the most popular neighborhoods to visit in Berlin:

Mitte

Mitte is the historical heart of Berlin and is home to many of the city's most famous landmarks and tourist attractions. It is located in the center of the city and is bordered by the Spree River to the north and east. Mitte is home to many museums, including Museum Island, as well as the iconic Brandenburg Gate and the Reichstag Building. The neighborhood is also known for its trendy cafes, boutique shops, and vibrant nightlife.

Kreuzberg

Kreuzberg is a vibrant and diverse neighborhood located in the southern part of Berlin. It is known for its multicultural population and is home to many artists, musicians, and creative types. Kreuzberg has a vibrant nightlife scene, with many bars, clubs, and music venues. The neighborhood is also home to several parks and green spaces, including the popular Görlitzer Park.

Friedrichshain

Friedrichshain is a trendy and hip neighborhood located in the eastern part of Berlin. It is known for its street art, cafes, and nightlife scene. Friedrichshain is home to several popular clubs and music venues, including the famous Berghain nightclub. The neighborhood is also home to several parks, including the popular Volkspark Friedrichshain.

Prenzlauer Berg

Prenzlauer Berg is a trendy and gentrified neighborhood located in the northern part of Berlin. It is known for its stylish cafes, boutique shops, and trendy bars. Prenzlauer Berg is home to several parks and green spaces, including Mauerpark and Kollwitzplatz. The neighborhood also has a thriving arts and culture scene, with several galleries and performance spaces. Prenzlauer Berg is a popular destination for young professionals and families and is known for its well-preserved historic architecture.

Neukölln

Neukölln is a multicultural and diverse neighborhood located in the southern part of Berlin. It is known for its vibrant and lively atmosphere, with many bars, cafes, and restaurants. Neukölln is home to several parks and green spaces, including the popular Tempelhofer Feld, a former airport turned park. The neighborhood also has a strong arts and culture scene, with several galleries and performance spaces. Neukölln has a reputation for being gritty and alternative, but it is also undergoing significant gentrification in recent years.

Charlottenburg-Wilmersdorf

Charlottenburg-Wilmersdorf is a upscale and affluent neighborhood located in the western part of Berlin. It is known for its elegant boulevards, high-end shopping, and luxurious residential areas. Charlottenburg-Wilmersdorf is home to several famous landmarks, including the Charlottenburg Palace and the Kurfürstendamm shopping street. The neighborhood also has several parks and green spaces, including the popular Tiergarten park. Charlottenburg-Wilmersdorf has a reputation for being posh and exclusive, with a high concentration of luxury hotels and restaurants.

Schöneberg

Schöneberg is a diverse and historic neighborhood located in the southern part of Berlin. It is known for its multicultural population, vibrant nightlife, and trendy cafes. Schöneberg is home to several historic landmarks, including the Rathaus Schöneberg, where John F. Kennedy gave his famous "Ich bin ein Berliner" speech. The neighborhood also has several parks and green spaces, including the popular Rudolph-Wilde-Park.

Schöneberg is a popular destination for young professionals and students, with several universities and educational institutions located in the area.

Wedding

Wedding is a multicultural and up-and-coming neighborhood located in the northern part of Berlin. It is known for its lively atmosphere, with many bars, cafes, and restaurants. Wedding is home to several parks and green spaces, including the popular Volkspark Rehberge. The neighborhood also has a growing arts and culture scene, with several galleries and performance spaces. Wedding is a popular destination for young artists and creatives, and is known for its affordable housing and diverse population.

Food and Drink in Berlin

Berlin is a vibrant and diverse city, and its cuisine reflects its multicultural population and rich history. From traditional German fare to international cuisine, there is no shortage of delicious food and drink options to explore in Berlin.

Traditional Berlin cuisine and specialties

vegetables. One of the most famous dishes in Berlin is the currywurst, a sausage served with a spicy tomato-based sauce and curry powder. Other popular traditional dishes include schnitzel, a breaded and fried cutlet of meat, and kartoffelpuffer, a potato pancake served with applesauce or sour cream.

For those with a sweet tooth, Berlin has several famous pastries and desserts, including the Berliner, a jelly-filled doughnut, and the Baumkuchen, a layered cake coated in chocolate.

In addition to traditional German cuisine, Berlin also has a thriving international food scene, with many restaurants serving cuisine from around the world. Some popular international cuisines in Berlin include Turkish, Vietnamese, and Middle Eastern.

Visitors to Berlin should also sample the city's famous beer and wine. Berlin has several famous breweries, including the Berliner Kindl and the Bierfabrik, and visitors can sample a variety of local beers at bars and restaurants throughout the city. For wine lovers, Berlin has several wine bars and shops specializing in German wines, as well as international wines from around the world.

Best places to try currywurst and other local foods

1. Curry 36: Located in the trendy Kreuzberg neighborhood, Curry 36 is one of the most famous currywurst stands in Berlin. The stand has been serving up delicious currywurst

for over 30 years and is a must-visit for any foodie in the city.

2. Konnopke's Imbiss: Another famous currywurst stand, Konnopke's Imbiss has been serving up delicious sausage since 1930. The stand is located near the famous Alexanderplatz and is a popular spot for locals and tourists alike.

3. Prater Garten: Prater Garten is a historic beer garden located in the Prenzlauer Berg neighborhood. In addition to serving up delicious German beer, the restaurant also has a menu of traditional German dishes, including schnitzel and kartoffelpuffer.

4. Curry & Chili: This small restaurant in the Schöneberg neighborhood specializes in currywurst and other German specialties. The restaurant has a cozy atmosphere and is a great spot to try traditional Berlin cuisine.

5. Mustafa's Gemüse Kebap: For those looking for something a bit different, Mustafa's Gemüse Kebap serves up delicious Turkish-style kebabs with a twist. The restaurant is located in the Kreuzberg neighborhood and is a popular spot for locals and tourists alike.

Berlin's craft beer scene and traditional bars
Craft Beer Scene:

Berlin has a thriving craft beer scene, with several microbreweries and taprooms located throughout the city. Many of these breweries specialize in traditional German beer styles, such as pilsners and hefeweizens, while others experiment with more innovative flavors and brewing techniques. Some of the best craft breweries and taprooms to visit in Berlin include **BRLO, Brewdog, and Vagabund Brauerei.** Visitors can also take a guided tour of some of

Berlin's best breweries and learn about the history and techniques of German brewing.

Traditional Bars:

In addition to its craft beer scene, Berlin is also home to several traditional bars and pubs. These bars offer a cozy and authentic atmosphere, with classic German decor and hearty pub food. Some of the best traditional bars to visit in Berlin include **Schwarzes Cafe**, a popular late-night spot in the Charlottenburg neighborhood, and **Klo**, a historic bar in the Mitte neighborhood known for its impressive selection of German beers. Visitors can also take a guided pub crawl through some of Berlin's best traditional bars and experience the city's famous nightlife scene.

Trendy cafes and cocktail bars

Trendy Cafes:

Berlin is known for its thriving cafe culture, with many trendy and hip cafes located throughout the city. These cafes offer a cozy and inviting atmosphere, with stylish decor and delicious food and drinks. Some of the best trendy cafes to visit in Berlin include The Barn, a specialty coffee shop with several locations throughout the city, and Roamers, a popular brunch spot in the Neukölln neighborhood. Visitors can also take a guided tour of some of Berlin's best cafes and learn about the history and techniques of German coffee culture.

Cocktail Bars:

Berlin also has a thriving cocktail scene, with several trendy bars and speakeasies located throughout the city. These bars offer a stylish and sophisticated atmosphere, with expertly crafted cocktails and inventive drink menus. Some of the best cocktail bars to visit in Berlin include **Buck and Breck**, a hidden bar in the Mitte neighborhood known for its innovative drinks and intimate atmosphere, and **Green Door**, a popular speakeasy in the Schöneberg neighborhood with a vintage feel. Visitors can also take a guided tour of some of Berlin's best cocktail bars and learn about the city's history of mixology.

Berlin is one of the most gastronomically satisfying places in Europe because of all of the immigration it's been having during the last decades mixed with the traditional German food. Here we provide you with some of our favorite dining places in the city:

1- **Vapiano** (*Postdamer Platz 5*):

Vapiano is an Italian restaurant which specializes in pasta. What makes this place different is that you have all the different ingredients right there to see and choose how it is that you want your pasta. Since you can see while your pasta is being cooked, you can ask them to put a bit more oil or salt to the sauce, or if you want fewer onions on your carbonara sauce, for example. They also serve delicious pizza!

2- **Konnopke Imbiss** (*Schönhauser Allee 44a*):

This is a mythic place in Berlin situated below the train rails of Schönhauser Allee stop. At first glance, it looks like any other fast food place, but if you pay attention you will notice that there's always a long queue of a lot of people eager to get their currywurst; this is because they are particularly tasty. They also serve Wiener, bockwurst, schnitzel and vegetarian currywurst.

3- **Die Berliner Republik** (*Schiffbauerdamm 8*):

Situated next to the Spree River, Die Berliner Republik is a huge local place, usually very crowded and full of TV's on you'll be able to see all kinds of sports. Despite its size, it still maintains the essence of a traditional German tavern. All of their foods is local traditional, and their beers offer is spectacular, with more than 20 different beers for you to choose from.

4- **The Bird** (*Am Falkplatz 5*):

The Bird is the best hamburger restaurant of Berlin. This American-style restaurant is located right behind Mauerpark. The burger's meat is top-notch quality, and the fries are surprisingly good. The two owners of this place are from New York and have really given it a hip Brooklyn-style.

5- **Habibi Imbiss** (*Goltzstraße 24*): If you're looking for the best falafel in Berlin, this is the place, and it's also one of the cheapest! Open until 3 AM during the week, and until 5 AM on weekends, Habibi Imbiss comes as the ideal location for those nocturnal fans of falafel, shawarmas, and hummus. The employees are so friendly that they even offer you a cup of tea while you wait for your food to be served.

If you're visiting a large city such as **Berlin**, a shopping afternoon may be a part of your planning. The good news is that this is a **very nice city to shop**: prices are more than reasonable, and most shops are easy to reach. Here we will mention the **best 5 areas in Berlin to go shopping**, and a short summary of each one of them:

1. Kurfürstendamm

This is a vast and famous street of West Berlin. It is most know for the department stores KaDeWe and Peek and Cloppenburg. The KaDeWe store alone is actually worth the visit: it consists of 60.000 m² of stores with products that go from clothing to cosmetics or furniture.

2. Alexa

Located at walking distance from Alexanderplatz within the Mitte neighborhood, Alexa is a great indoor shopping center. It has a total of 180 different stores and is very centrally located, making it very convenient to visit. It also counts with 17 different restaurants for you to have a meal if you're planning on spending many hours shopping.

3. Mall of Berlin

The newest area to go shopping at in Berlin! The Mall of Berlin opened in 2014, with more than 200,000 square meters of stores! It is very conveniently located as well, next to Potsdamer

Platz. At The Mall of Berlin, you'll find brands such as Armani, Hugo Boss, Guess, Replay, H&M, Zara, C&A, Peek & Cloppenburg or Saturn, among many others.

4. Hackescher Markt

The certain area to go shopping for Berliner youth and students. Here you may find brands such as Diesel, Adidas or Pepe Jeans. You can also combine your visit with some drinks or a dinner, as the area is full of many good and cheap restaurants and bars.

Nightlife in Berlin

Berlin is arguably the city with the most important night scene in the world, so it becomes tough to know where to go when you have so many different options. Here we provide you with a guide to our favorite bars and clubs in Berlin so that you don't get lost between that great city's nightlife. Remember that Berliners go out really late at night, so the recommended times for each place are: bars between 9 PM and 2 AM and clubs after 2 AM.

Berlin bars:

- **The Bar Marqués** (Graefestraße 92, Kreuzberg): Located in Kreuzberg neighborhood, this bar will give you the impression of going through a time machine right to the 1920's. The cocktails are excellent and original.
- **Die Weinerei** (*Veteranenstrasse 14, Mitte*): For only 2 euros you get a glass and are invited to drink as much wine as you like. After you had enough wine, you can leave as much money as you consider fair for the tip's jar. This is a new concept that of course can get easily abused, but there is a great atmosphere that inspires trust at this place, and it actually works.
- **Barbie Deinhoff's** (*Schlesische Strasse 16, Kreuzberg*): Barbie Deinhoff's attracts people from all kinds of tendencies: sophisticated transsexuals, artists, local intellectuals and college students. The place is managed by Lena Braun, a famous local drag queen. Drinks are very cheap, and the place also offers a 2x1 happy hour every day from 6 PM to 9 PM.
- **Bei Schlawinchen** (*Schönleinstrasse 34, Kreuzberg*): A great place to go to if you're interested in getting out of the touristic flow for a while and feel like a local Berliner. Bei Schlawinchen is opened 24/7 and prices are very economical as well.

Berlin nightclubs:

- **Berghain** *(Am Bahnhof Wriezener, 10243)*:

Opened in 2004, this club is considered by many as the best in the world. It is also one of the most exclusive ones, not because of the price of the entrance, but because of how difficult it is to get in. There are even blogs dedicated to understanding how to get into Berghain, but the truth is that no one really knows: security at the door may or may not let you in based on random reasons. It has nothing to do with glamor or exclusivity, since, for example, the club got worldwide attention for not letting Paris Hilton in a few years ago.

If you do find your way in, you'll find a former electric station with an 18 meters high roof, and some of the best techno music you can find.

Entrance Price: 14€

- **Tresor** *(Köpenicker Straße 70)*:

This is another famous clandestine underground club that is totally worth a visit. Founded in 1991, the club was installed within one of the biggest old markets of Berlin. Since 2007, they relocated to this former abandoned electric station (just like Berghain).

Entrance Price: 6-12€

- **KitKat Club** *(Köpenicker Straße 76)*:

Inspired by 1930's burlesque, Austrian cineaste Simon Thaur founded KitKat Club in 1994. This place is very famous for its *sexually uninhibited* parties. Nowadays, KitKat Club is one of the most recognized and visited places of the techno movement, attracting tourists from all over Europe. To get in, you will have to respect the hilarious dress-code, which consists of glamorous, fetishist clothing.

Entrance Price: 15€

Day Trips from Berlin

While Berlin has plenty to offer visitors, there are also many exciting day trip destinations located just outside the city. From picturesque castles to charming towns, there are many unique and fascinating destinations within easy reach of Berlin. Visitors can take a break from the hustle and bustle of the city and explore the surrounding countryside, learning about the history and culture of the region. Whether by car, train, or bus, there are many day trips from Berlin that are easily accessible and offer a chance to see a different side of Germany.

Potsdam

Located just 25 kilometers southwest of Berlin, the city of Potsdam makes for a perfect day trip destination. Known for its stunning architecture, beautiful parks, and fascinating history, Potsdam is a must-visit for anyone interested in exploring the region around Berlin.

Getting there: Potsdam is easily accessible from Berlin by train, with regular service from several stations throughout the city. The journey takes about 30-40 minutes and prices start at around €3.50 one way. Visitors can also take a guided tour from Berlin that includes transportation to and from Potsdam, as well as a tour of the city's main sights.

One-day travel itinerary:

1. Start your day by visiting the iconic Sanssouci Palace, a stunning rococo-style palace and gardens built by Frederick the Great in the 18th century. The palace is a UNESCO World Heritage Site and is surrounded by beautiful gardens and fountains.

2. Next, visit the Neues Palais, a grand baroque-style palace built in the 18th century as a summer residence for the Prussian royal family. The palace has a stunning collection of artwork and is surrounded by beautiful gardens.

3. After touring the palaces, head to the charming Dutch Quarter, a neighborhood in the heart of Potsdam with beautiful 17th-century architecture. The neighborhood is home to several shops, cafes, and restaurants, and is a great place to stop for lunch.

4. In the afternoon, head to the beautiful Sanssouci Park, a sprawling park filled with gardens, statues, and beautiful views. Take a stroll through the park and visit the Chinese House, a stunning pavilion built in the 18th century and inspired by Chinese design.

5. Finally, end your day by visiting the Cecilienhof Palace, a beautiful palace built in the early 20th century and famous for hosting the Potsdam Conference in 1945. The palace has a fascinating history and is surrounded by beautiful gardens and parkland.

Useful websites:

- https://www.potsdamtourismus.de/en/

- https://www.spsg.de/en/home/

- https://www.bvg.de/en

- https://www.viator.com/Berlin-tours/Day-Trips-and-Excursions/d488-g5

Visitors to Potsdam should plan to spend a full day exploring the city's many sights and attractions. Tickets to the palaces and gardens can be purchased in advance online or at the entrance, and visitors can save money by purchasing a combination ticket. The city is easy to explore on foot, but visitors can also rent bikes or take a guided tour for a more in-depth experience.

Dresden

Located about 200 kilometers south of Berlin, the city of Dresden is a beautiful and historic city that makes for a perfect day trip destination. Known for its stunning architecture, cultural attractions, and beautiful setting along the Elbe River, Dresden is a must-visit for anyone exploring the region around Berlin.

Getting there: Dresden is easily accessible from Berlin by train, with regular service from several stations throughout the city. The journey takes about 2 hours and prices start at around €25 one way. Visitors can also take a guided tour from Berlin that includes transportation to and from Dresden, as well as a tour of the city's main sights.

One-day travel itinerary:

1. Start your day by visiting the **Zwinger Palace**, a stunning baroque-style palace that houses several museums and galleries. The palace is surrounded by beautiful gardens and fountains and is a great place to explore Dresden's rich cultural heritage.

2. Next, visit the **Frauenkirche**, a beautiful church in the heart of the city that was destroyed during World War II and painstakingly rebuilt in the years following. The church has a fascinating history and is a testament to the resilience and determination of the people of Dresden.

3. After touring the church, head to the **Dresden Castle**, a grand palace built in the 16th century that now houses several museums and galleries. The palace has a stunning collection of artwork and is surrounded by beautiful gardens and parkland.

4. In the afternoon, head to the **Neumarkt**, a beautiful square in the heart of the city that is home to several historic buildings and monuments. The square is a great place to stop for lunch and soak up the atmosphere of the city.

5. Finally, end your day by visiting the **Elbe River**, which runs through the heart of Dresden and is a beautiful spot to take a stroll and enjoy the city's natural beauty.

Useful websites:

- https://www.dresden.de/en/tourism/tourism.php

- https://www.skd.museum/en/home/

- https://www.bahn.com/en/view/index.shtml

- https://www.viator.com/Berlin-tours/Day-Trips-and-Excursions/d488-g5

Visitors to Dresden should plan to spend a full day exploring the city's many sights and attractions. Tickets to the museums and galleries can be purchased in advance online or at the entrance, and visitors can save money by purchasing a combination ticket. The city is easy to explore on foot, but visitors can also rent bikes or take a guided tour for a more in-depth experience.

Hamburg

Located about 280 kilometers northwest of Berlin, the city of Hamburg is a vibrant and lively city that makes for a perfect day trip destination. Known for its beautiful harbor, stunning architecture, and rich cultural heritage, Hamburg is a must-visit for anyone exploring the region around Berlin.

Getting there:

Hamburg is easily accessible from Berlin by train, with regular service from several stations throughout the city. The journey takes about 2-3 hours and prices start at around **€29** one way. Visitors can also take a guided tour from Berlin that includes transportation to and from Hamburg, as well as a tour of the city's main sights.

One-day travel itinerary:

1. Start your day by visiting the **Elbphilharmonie**, a stunning concert hall located in the heart of Hamburg's

harbor. The building is a masterpiece of modern architecture and offers stunning views of the city and the river.

2. Next, visit the **St. Michaelis Church**, a beautiful baroque-style church that is one of the most recognizable landmarks in Hamburg. Visitors can climb to the top of the church tower for panoramic views of the city.

3. After touring the church, head to the **Speicherstadt**, a historic district of warehouses and canals that is now home to several museums and galleries. The district has a fascinating history and is a testament to Hamburg's importance as a port city.

4. In the afternoon, head to the **Hamburger Kunsthalle**, one of the largest and most important art museums in Germany. The museum has a stunning collection of artwork from throughout history and is a must-visit for any art lover.

5. Finally, end your day by visiting the **Fish Market**, a bustling market that takes place every Sunday morning and is a popular spot for locals and tourists alike. The market is known for its fresh seafood and lively atmosphere.

Useful websites:

- https://www.hamburg.com/

- https://www.elbphilharmonie.de/en/

- https://www.st-michaelis.de/en/

- https://www.hamburg.de/speicherstadt/

- https://www.hamburger-kunsthalle.de/en/home

- https://www.hamburg.com/sights/fish-market/

Visitors to Hamburg should plan to spend a full day exploring the city's many sights and attractions. Tickets to the museums and galleries can be purchased in advance online or at the entrance, and visitors can save money by purchasing a combination ticket. The city is easy to explore on foot or by public transportation, and visitors can also take a guided tour for a more in-depth experience.

Leipzig

Located about 160 kilometers southwest of Berlin, the city of Leipzig is a charming and historic city that makes for a perfect day trip destination. Known for its rich cultural heritage, beautiful parks, and lively music scene, Leipzig is a must-visit for anyone exploring the region around Berlin.

Getting there:

Leipzig is easily accessible from Berlin by train, with regular service from several stations throughout the city. The journey takes about 1-2 hours and prices start at around **€16** one way. Visitors can also take a guided tour from Berlin that includes transportation to and from Leipzig, as well as a tour of the city's main sights.

One-day travel itinerary:

1. Start your day by visiting the **St. Thomas Church**, a beautiful church in the heart of Leipzig that is famous for its connection to Johann Sebastian Bach. The church has a fascinating history and is a testament to Leipzig's rich musical heritage.

2. Next, visit the **Leipzig Market Square**, a beautiful square in the heart of the city that is home to several historic buildings and monuments. The square is a great place to stop for lunch and soak up the atmosphere of the city.

3. After touring the square, head to the **Museum in der Runden Ecke**, a fascinating museum that is dedicated to the history of the Stasi, the secret police of East Germany. The museum has a large collection of artifacts and

documents and is a must-visit for anyone interested in the history of the Cold War.

4. In the afternoon, head to the **Leipzig Zoo**, one of the oldest and most important zoos in Germany. The zoo has a stunning collection of animals from all over the world and is a great place to spend an afternoon.

5. Finally, end your day by visiting the **Leipzig Panometer**, a unique museum that uses a 360-degree panoramic image to transport visitors back in time. The museum has a fascinating collection of historical images and is a must-visit for anyone interested in the history of Leipzig.

Useful websites:

- https://english.leipzig.de/

- https://www.thomaskirche.org/en/

- https://www.leipzig.de/en/leisure-culture-and-tourism/markets/markt/

- https://www.runde-ecke-leipzig.de/en/

- https://www.zoo-leipzig.de/en/

- https://panometer.de/leipzig/en/home/

Visitors to Leipzig should plan to spend a full day exploring the city's many sights and attractions. Tickets to the museums and galleries can be purchased in advance online or at the entrance, and visitors can save money by purchasing a combination ticket. The city is easy to explore on foot or by public transportation, and visitors can also take a guided tour for a more in-depth experience.

Spreewald

Located about 100 kilometers southeast of Berlin, the Spreewald is a unique and picturesque area of wetlands, forests, and waterways that makes for a perfect day trip destination. Known for its natural beauty, rich history, and traditional way of life, the Spreewald is a must-visit for anyone exploring the region around Berlin.

Getting there:

The easiest way to reach the Spreewald is by car, as public transportation options are limited. Visitors can rent a car or take a guided tour that includes transportation to and from the Spreewald, as well as a tour of the area's main sights.

One-day travel itinerary:

1. Start your day by taking a leisurely boat tour through the canals and waterways of the Spreewald. The tours offer a unique perspective on the area's natural beauty and are a great way to see the traditional houses and farms that dot the landscape.

2. Next, visit the **Slavic Fort of Raddusch**, a historic fortress built by the Slavic people more than 1,000 years ago. The fortress has a fascinating history and is a testament to the area's long and rich cultural heritage.

3. After touring the fortress, head to the **Spreewald Museum**, a small museum that is dedicated to the history and culture of the Spreewald. The museum has a fascinating collection of artifacts and documents and is a must-visit for anyone interested in the area's unique way of life.

4. In the afternoon, head to the **Bismarck Tower**, a historic tower that offers stunning views of the Spreewald and the surrounding countryside. The tower is a great place to take a break and enjoy the natural beauty of the area.

5. Finally, end your day by visiting one of the area's traditional restaurants or cafes, where you can sample local specialties like **Spreewald pickles** or **Spreewald gherkins**. These

delicious pickled cucumbers are a local specialty and are a must-try for any visitor to the Spreewald.

Useful websites:

- https://www.spreewald.de/en/

- https://www.spreewaldmuseum.de/en/

- https://www.bismarcktuerme.net/bismarcktuerme/216/spreewaldturm

Visitors to the Spreewald should plan to spend a full day exploring the area's many sights and attractions. Boat tours can be booked in advance or on the day of the trip, and visitors can save money by purchasing a combination ticket for the Spreewald Museum and other attractions. The area is best explored on foot or by boat, and visitors should be sure to bring comfortable shoes and clothing suitable for the outdoors.

A 3-Day Travel Itinerary for First Timers

9:00 - Arrival at **Berlin Tegel Airport (TXL) or Berlin Schönefeld Airport (SFX)**

At 9:00, you will arrive at either Berlin Tegel Airport (TXL) or Berlin Schönefeld Airport (SFX). Both airports have several options for transportation into the city center, including trains, buses, and taxis. For detailed instructions on how to get from the airport to the center of Berlin, refer to the "Getting to and Around Berlin" chapter of this guide.

Cost: 5€ approx. *Train or Bus*

9:30

We recommend staying in the **Mitte** neighborhood as it is centrally located and home to many of the city's most popular tourist attractions. The cost of transportation from the airport to the city center is approximately 5€ for either train or bus.

10:15

At 10:15, you will arrive at your hotel in Mitte. We recommend checking in and taking some time to rest and freshen up after your flight before embarking on your 3-day journey across Berlin.

If you arrive early and are eager to start exploring, you could drop off your bags at the hotel and head out to explore some of the nearby attractions. The Mitte neighborhood is home to many historic landmarks, including the Berlin Wall Memorial and the Reichstag building, as well as trendy cafes, restaurants, and shops.

We also recommend picking up a Berlin WelcomeCard, which offers discounts on public transportation and admission to many of the city's top attractions. This can be purchased at the airport or at any tourist information center in the city.

Overall, arriving in Berlin and getting settled in your hotel is an exciting start to your adventure in this vibrant and historic city. Take some time to relax and prepare for the adventures to come over the next few days.

11:00 - Head to Pariser Platz - Brandenburg Gate.

At 11:00, we recommend heading to Pariser Platz to visit the iconic Brandenburg Gate. This historic landmark is located in the heart of the old Mitte neighborhood, making it the perfect starting point for exploring the city's rich history and culture.

The Brandenburg Gate is one of the most famous and recognizable landmarks in Berlin, serving as a symbol of the city's resilience and unity. It was originally built in the late 18th century as a symbol of peace and now stands as a powerful reminder of Germany's tumultuous past and bright future.

While at Pariser Platz, take the time to explore the surrounding area, which is home to many other important landmarks, such as the Reichstag building and the Memorial to the Murdered Jews of Europe.

For more information on the history and significance of the Brandenburg Gate, refer to ZoomTip 1.1 in this guide. We also recommend taking a guided tour of the area, which will provide additional context and insight into the significance of these historic landmarks.

Overall, a visit to the Brandenburg Gate and Pariser Platz is a must-do for any visitor to Berlin. It's a great way to start your journey through the city and gain a deeper understanding of its rich history and culture.

11:30

After visiting the Brandenburg Gate and Pariser Platz, continue your tour around Mitte with a visit to the Memorial to the Murdered Jews of Europe. This powerful and moving monument is located just a short walk from the Brandenburg Gate and serves as a somber reminder of one of the darkest periods in human history.

The Memorial to the Murdered Jews of Europe is a vast and solemn space filled with over 2,700 gray rectangular blocks of varying heights. Visitors are encouraged to walk among the blocks and contemplate the enormity of the tragedy that occurred during the Holocaust.

For more information on the history and significance of the Memorial to the Murdered Jews of Europe, refer to ZoomTip

1.2 in this guide. We recommend taking the time to fully experience the monument and pay your respects to the victims of this horrific event.

After visiting the memorial, you could continue your tour of Mitte by exploring some of the area's many museums and galleries. The Museum Island, which we recommended earlier in this guide, is home to some of the city's most important cultural institutions, including the Pergamon Museum and the Neues Museum.

Alternatively, you could explore some of the area's trendy cafes and restaurants or take a stroll through the nearby Hackescher Markt, a bustling square filled with shops, street performers, and historic architecture.

Overall, exploring Mitte is a great way to get a sense of the history and culture of Berlin. With its many landmarks, museums, and cultural institutions, there is something for everyone in this vibrant and historic neighborhood.

12:30 - Visit the **Reichstag Building**.

The famous Reichstag dome, German Parliament, is work of Norman Foster and is definitely worth a visit. Its roof terrace offers incredible views of the congressional and government district. Please consider that the entrance is free, but to enter the Reichstag, you need to make a reservation through this website.

13:30

Grab something to eat and rest for a while. We suggest you try the famous and traditional currywurst since this is your first meal in Berlin.

14:30 - Take a long walk around Tier Garten.

At 14:30, we recommend taking a long walk around the beautiful Tiergarten park. This expansive green space is located in the heart of Berlin, right next to the Reichstag Building, and offers a peaceful respite from the hustle and bustle of the city.

As you explore Tiergarten, you'll be amazed by the park's natural beauty and tranquility. The park is home to numerous walking paths, gardens, and lakes, as well as several notable monuments and sculptures.

One must-see attraction in Tiergarten is the Victory Column, a towering structure that offers stunning views of the surrounding area. The column can be accessed via a spiral staircase, but visitors should be warned that the climb is quite steep.

For those who prefer a more leisurely pace, there are plenty of benches and picnic areas throughout the park where you can relax and enjoy the scenery. You may even spot some wildlife, as Tiergarten is home to a variety of birds and other animals.

Overall, a visit to Tiergarten is a great way to get some fresh air and take in the natural beauty of Berlin. Whether you choose to walk, jog, bike, or simply relax, there's something for everyone in this expansive and picturesque park.

15:30 - See the Berlin Victory Column.

At 15:30, we recommend taking a closer look at the Berlin Victory Column while exploring Tiergarten. This historic monument is a must-see for anyone interested in the history and culture of Berlin.

The Berlin Victory Column, also known as the Siegessäule in German, was erected in the late 19th century to commemorate several significant Prussian military victories, including battles against Austria, Denmark, and Napoleon.

The column itself stands at over 200 feet tall and is adorned with a variety of intricate sculptures and decorations, including a golden statue of the goddess Victoria at the top.

Visitors can climb to the top of the column via a spiral staircase, which offers breathtaking views of the surrounding area. However, it should be noted that the climb is quite steep and may not be suitable for everyone.

In addition to its historical significance, the Berlin Victory Column is also a popular destination for tourists and locals alike, offering a unique and memorable photo opportunity against the backdrop of the Tiergarten park.

Overall, a visit to the Berlin Victory Column is a must-do for anyone exploring Tiergarten or the surrounding area. Whether you're interested in history, architecture, or simply enjoying the stunning views, this iconic landmark is sure to leave a lasting impression.

16:15 - Visit the Topography of Terror Museum.

This particular museum is located where the Gestapo and SS headquarters used to be. It's a free, massive and dense museum, but it's totally worth the visit.

It also features an outdoors exhibition of which some fragments of the Berlin Wall are preserved, and an indoor exhibition on which you can observe, year after year, all kinds of histories, images and information about the horrors that took place from 1933 to 1945.

18:00 - Go to CheckPoint Charlie.

This was the most important border passing of the Berlin wall and constituted the crossing from the American control point to the Soviet one. See *ZoomTip 1.3* for knowing more about CheckPoint Charlie.

19:00 - Go to Postdamer Platz, a beautiful commercial and cultural spot of Berlin that is a must while you're visiting the city.

This specific corner is also known for having installed the first traffic light in Europe.

20:00 - Head back to the hotel.

21:00

At 21:00, we recommend winding down after a long day of sightseeing by having dinner at a nearby restaurant and then returning to your hotel for some well-deserved rest.

There are plenty of excellent dining options in Berlin, ranging from traditional German cuisine to international favorites. We recommend doing some research beforehand to find a restaurant that suits your taste and budget.

After dinner, take some time to relax and recharge for the next day's adventures. While you may have covered a lot of ground on your first day in Berlin, there is still so much more to see and do in this vibrant and historic city.

Consider planning out your itinerary for the next day, or simply take some time to reflect on the sights and experiences of the day before. Whatever you choose to do, be sure to get a good night's sleep so that you're ready to tackle whatever comes your way on your second day in Berlin.

1st Day in Berlin - Map

Below you will find the maps corresponding to all the different places we've recommended for your first day at Berlin. They are accessible in Google Maps format for you to easily use on your smartphone or tablet while you are in Berlin.

As you can see on the map, we've only covered the Mitte area, so there's much more to know during your second and third day!

Get this map online: click here or visit bit.ly/BerlinFirstDay

The **Brandenburg Gate** is an old entrance gate to Berlin and one of the most significant symbols of the city and of the entire country as well. It's located at Pariser Platz, marking the end of Unter den Linden Avenue and setting the beginning of the Tie Garten. The Gate is 26 meters high, 65 meters wide and 11 meters long, and was made by the architect Carl Gotthard Langhans.

Brandenburg Gate enjoyed much tranquility until the Second World War, which caused several damages to its structure and nearly destroyed it. In 1956, both sides of the city (East and West) joined forces for attempting to reconstruct the gate. But in 1961, after the construction of the Berlin Wall, the gate became trapped between both sides, not belonging to the East but neither the West, so basically no one had access to it.

Following the city's reunification, the Brandenburg Gate finally got back to the place it deserved as the city's more significant monument.

The Memorial to the Murdered Jews of Europe, also known as Holocaust Memorial, is a monument designed for remembering and honoring the Jews victims of the Holocaust. Designed by architect Peter Eisenman and engineer Buro Happold, the construction was started in April 2003 and finished in December 2004.

This is indeed a very curious and particular monument. It primarily consists of 2711 concrete gray bricks of different heights and sizes. According to Eisenman project, the bricks are designed for producing an uncomfortable and confusing atmosphere; the entire monument tries to represent a system that is supposedly in order, but that has lost complete touch with human reason.

Checkpoint Charlie was the most famous of the border crossings of the Berlin Wall from 1945 to 1990. It opened the passage to go from West to East Berlin, from which are today the neighborhoods of Mitte and Kreuzberg.

Its usage was allowed only to the army or embassy members. In 1961, the SED attempted to restrain the rights that Occidental major powers had in Berlin. As a result, in October 1961, both Soviet and American tanks remained confronted with heavy ammo at Checkpoint Charlie.

This place was also scenario to some of the most dramatic escapes from Eastern Berlin; some of them even tragic, such as the death of Peter Fechter in 1962.

9:00 - Go to Sachsenhausen Concentration Camp.

At 9:00, we recommend visiting Sachsenhausen Concentration Camp, located just outside of Berlin. While this visit may be difficult for some due to the atrocities committed there during World War II, we believe it is an important opportunity to learn about and reflect on the experiences of the victims.

To get to Sachsenhausen, take the S1 Metro line up to Oranienburg. The ride takes approximately 45 minutes. Once you arrive in Oranienburg, you have two options: you can either walk for about 20 minutes to reach the concentration camp or take a bus that stops outside the Oranienburg station.

Once you arrive at Sachsenhausen, you will have the opportunity to explore the site and learn about its history through exhibits, memorials, and guided tours. While it can be a sobering and emotional experience, visiting Sachsenhausen can be a powerful way to pay tribute to the victims and ensure that the lessons of the past are not forgotten.

For more information on Sachsenhausen Concentration Camp, see ZoomTip 2.1. We recommend allowing several hours for your visit to the camp, and taking the time to reflect on the experience afterwards.

13:00 - Go back to the central part of Berlin with the S1 metro line and grab something to eat.

14:00 - Go to the East Side Gallery.

At 14:00, we recommend visiting the East Side Gallery, a must-see attraction for any art lover or history enthusiast. To get there, take the subway to Warschauer St. station.

The East Side Gallery is an open-air gallery that stretches over a kilometer along the famous Berlin Wall. Here, you can admire an impressive collection of street art murals and graffiti, many of which reference the fall of the Wall and the reunification of Germany. The East Side Gallery is a living testament to the resilience and creativity of the human spirit in the face of adversity.

Be sure to check out ZoomTip 2.2 for more information on the East Side Gallery, including tips for exploring the gallery and its fascinating history. Don't forget to bring your camera, as there are many photo-worthy moments to capture along the way.

After exploring the East Side Gallery, consider taking a leisurely stroll through the nearby neighborhoods of Friedrichshain or Kreuzberg, which are known for their vibrant street art scene, lively cafes, and eclectic shops. Or, if you're feeling up for it, hop on a bike and explore the city on two wheels. Berlin is a great city for biking, with plenty of bike lanes and scenic routes to choose from.

16:30 - Go to Alexanderplatz.

At 16:30, we suggest heading to Alexanderplatz, another popular hub in the heart of Berlin. Take a moment to sit on the steps and people-watch, as this bustling square is a hub of activity and a great spot for observing daily life in the city.

One of the highlights of Alexanderplatz is the famous World Clock, which displays the time in many different parts of the world. Take a closer look and you may notice that the clock also features information on the distances between different cities, making it a useful tool for global travelers.

Beyond the World Clock, Alexanderplatz is also home to many shops, restaurants, and entertainment options. Be sure to check out ZoomTip 2.3 for more information on what to see and do in the area.

If you have some extra time and energy, consider taking a trip up to the top of the nearby Fernsehturm (TV tower), which offers stunning panoramic views of the city. Note that this attraction can be busy, so it's best to book tickets in advance or arrive early to beat the crowds.

18:00

Head back to the hotel and rest for a while to prepare for experiencing Berlin nightlife.

19:30

At 19:30, we suggest beginning your evening by indulging in some of the amazing food options available in Berlin. Check out the "Our Favorite Dining Places in Berlin" chapter for recommendations on where to go for delicious meals and drinks.

Whether you're in the mood for traditional German cuisine, international flavors, or trendy new spots, Berlin has something to offer every palate. Take your time savoring the flavors and enjoying the ambiance of your chosen restaurant or bar, soaking up the unique atmosphere that only Berlin can offer.

After dinner, consider checking out some of the city's nightlife options. From chic cocktail bars to lively clubs, Berlin has a vibrant and diverse scene that caters to all tastes. Check out ZoomTip 3.3 for more information on where to go for a memorable night out in the city.

21:00 - Go to Kreuzberg neighborhood.

At 21:00, we recommend heading over to the vibrant and eclectic Kreuzberg neighborhood. Here, you'll find a lively bar scene with plenty of options for delicious beer and cocktails.

Start your tour at Graefestraße, one of the central streets in Kreuzberg. Some of our top recommendations for bars in this area include The Bar Marqués, Barbie Deinhoff's, Brauhaus Südstern, and Salon Schmück.

If you're looking for more options, be sure to check out the "Nightlife in Berlin" chapter for even more recommendations on where to start your night out. Whether you're in the mood for a cozy pub atmosphere or a trendy cocktail bar, Kreuzberg has something to offer every taste. So grab a drink and immerse yourself in the unique atmosphere of this dynamic neighborhood.

After midnight

If you still have some energy and are up for some more adventure after a night of drinking German beers, it's time to explore Berlin's famous nightclub scene! Keep in mind that Berlin's clubbing scene starts quite late, usually after 2 AM, so try not to go too early and miss out on the best parts.

Berlin is known as the nightlife capital of Europe, and possibly even the world, with some of the most incredible nightclubs you can find. If you're into techno, don't miss the opportunity to experience some of the legendary clubs, like Tresor or the internationally renowned Berghain. For more information on these epic nightclubs, check out the "Nightlife in Berlin" chapter.

2nd Day in Berlin - Map

Below you will find the maps corresponding to all the different activities that we recommend for your second day in Berlin. They are accessible in Google Maps format for you to easily use on your smartphone or tablet while you are in Berlin.

Get this map online: click here or visit bit.ly/BerlinSecondDay

The Sachsenhausen Concentration Camp is a dark reminder of the atrocities committed during the Nazi regime. It was built in 1936, on the outskirts of Berlin, with the aim of confining and exterminating political opponents, Jews, gypsies, homosexuals, and others considered "undesirables" by the regime. It is estimated that over 30,000 people lost their lives in this camp, either by execution, starvation, disease, or forced labor.

While visiting Sachsenhausen is not a typical tourist attraction, it is an essential journey that can help visitors gain a deeper understanding of the horrors of the Holocaust. The experience can be overwhelming for some, as it confronts the darkest aspects of humanity. Nevertheless, we believe that it is important to remember these events to ensure they are never repeated.

During the visit, you will have the chance to explore the different areas of the camp, including the prisoners' quarters, the barracks, the prison, the kitchen, Tower E, the infirmary barracks, and the T-building. Each area offers a glimpse into the daily lives of the prisoners and the inhumane conditions they endured. The guides on-site are knowledgeable and can provide additional information to deepen your understanding of this tragic part of history.

One of the most popular attractions in Berlin is the East Side Gallery, which is recognized as an international symbol of freedom. It was established in 1990 and is made up of 1316 meters of murals painted on a section of the Berlin Wall. The gallery features 105 different artworks created by artists from all over the world.

The East Side Gallery showcases a wide range of styles and themes, including political messages, pop culture references, and abstract designs. Some of the notable artists who contributed to the gallery include Dimitri Vrubel, Bodo Sperling, Siegfried Santoni, Kasra Alavi, Jim Avignon, and Thierry Noir. Walking through this outdoor gallery is like taking a journey through different cultures and ideas.

Make sure to bring your camera as you walk along the gallery, capturing the most impressive pieces of art. Some of the most famous murals that you should definitely keep an eye out for include "My God, Help Me to Survive This Deadly Love" by Dimitri Vrubel, "The Wall Jumper" by Thierry Noir, and "Test the Rest" by Birgit Kinder.

It's free to visit the East Side Gallery, so don't miss this chance to experience an important part of Berlin's history and culture.

10:00 - Take a walk from the hotel to the Museum Island.

At 10:00, we recommend taking a leisurely stroll from your hotel to the Museum Island, a must-visit destination for any art or history lover. Located on an island in the River Spree, this extraordinary ensemble of five different museums showcases some of the world's most important collections of art and artifacts.

The five museums on Berlin's Museum Island are the Bode Museum, Pergamon Museum, Neues Museum, Alte Nationalgalerie, and Altes Museum. Each museum has its own unique focus, from ancient artifacts and sculptures to modern art and paintings. We highly recommend taking the time to explore at least one or two of these world-class museums during your visit.

As you walk through the heart of Berlin's city center, take in the stunning architecture and history of the area. The Museum Island is also home to the Berlin Cathedral, a magnificent 19th-century cathedral that dominates the island's skyline.

If you're not sure which museum to visit, see ZoomTip 3.1 for more information on each of the museums and their collections. The Museum Island is a must-see destination for anyone visiting Berlin, and a morning stroll through this historic and cultural hub is the perfect way to start your day.

13:30 - Grab something to eat and go to Tempelhof Park.

At 13:30, we suggest grabbing a bite to eat and heading over to Tempelhof Park for a truly unique experience. While you can get there with the U6 metro and getting off at the U Kaiserin-Augusta Str station, we recommend against walking the entire way from the Museum Island as it can be quite a distance. Instead, save your energy for exploring the park once you arrive.

Tempelhof Park is unlike any other public park you may have visited before, as it was once a fully functioning international airport until its closure in 2008. In a bold move, the city decided to convert this vast space into a public park, leaving the airport infrastructure and runways intact. This means that visitors can explore the park and enjoy hundreds of square meters of wide-open space and tranquility, all while surrounded by the remnants of the airport's past.

It's a fascinating blend of history, nature, and urban space that makes Tempelhof Park one of the most unique public parks in the world. Since its opening in 2010, just two years after the airport closure, it has become the largest public park in Berlin and a popular destination for locals and tourists alike.

You can bring a picnic or grab a snack at one of the food trucks or cafes located throughout the park. Take a stroll or bike ride along the old runways, explore the community gardens, or even try your hand at kitesurfing on the large open spaces. There's no shortage of things to do and see at Tempelhof Park.

Whether you're a history buff, nature lover, or simply looking for a unique and peaceful escape from the bustle of the city, Tempelhof Park is a must-visit destination in Berlin.

16:30

At 16:30, after a relaxing and contemplative walk through Tempelhof Feld Park, take the U6 metro back to the city center and head back to your hotel to prepare for your departure.

However, if you're not ready to leave just yet, there are plenty of other activities to enjoy during your last few hours in Berlin. You could explore some of the trendy neighborhoods, such as Kreuzberg or Friedrichshain, and enjoy some of the local bars and restaurants. Or, you could visit some of the city's famous landmarks, such as the Brandenburg Gate or Checkpoint Charlie.

If you're looking for a more relaxing activity, why not head to one of the city's many spas or wellness centers? Berlin is known for its thriving wellness industry and there are plenty of options to choose from, whether you prefer a traditional sauna experience or a more modern spa treatment.

For those with an interest in the arts, you could visit one of the many galleries or theaters in the city. Berlin has a rich and vibrant art scene, with many exhibitions and performances taking place throughout the year.

Alternatively, if you're a foodie, why not take a culinary tour of the city and try some of the delicious local cuisine? Berlin is home to many Michelin-starred restaurants as well as street food markets and food trucks, so there's something for every taste and budget.

At 18:00, it's time to collect your luggage and head to the airport. If you have time, you could grab a bite to eat at one of the many restaurants or cafes located within the airport before boarding your flight. We hope you had a wonderfu

3rd Day in Berlin – Map

Below you will find the maps corresponding to all the different activities that we recommend for your third day in Berlin. They are accessible in Google Maps format for you to easily use on your smartphone or tablet while you are in Berlin.

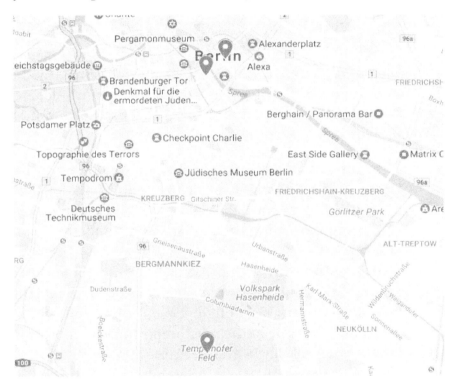

Get this map online

Declared as a Human Heritage place by UNESCO, the Museum Island is one of the most prestigious museum's ensembles in the world. The five institutions that together form the Museum Island are:

- **Pergamon Museum**: Opened in 1930, this is the most important and significant of the 5 museums of the island. The building has a Babylonia aspect and shows collections of Antiquities, the Oriental Museum, and the Islamic Art Museum.
- **Altes Museum:** The Altes Museum holds a Classic Antiquities collection which looks back to about 300 years in the past. It was built between 1823 and 1830 and is considered as one of the most important architectonic works of the classical Berlin architecture.
- **Neues Museum:** It was originally built between 1843 and 1855, but was severely damaged during WW2 and almost disappeared. It was reconstructed in 1997 by British architect David Chipperfield.
- **Alte Nationalgalerie:** Neo-classical building opened in 1876. It holds a 19th Century Art Collection.
- **Bode Museum:** Bode Museum was opened in 1904, and holds mostly sculptures collections.

One-Day Itinerary: Highlights of Berlin

If you only have one day to spend in Berlin, this itinerary will take you to some of the city's most famous landmarks and must-see attractions. Start the day early, around 08:00, to make the most of your time in the city.

Morning: Begin your day at the iconic Brandenburg Gate, located in the heart of the city. This neoclassical monument is a symbol of Germany's reunification and is one of the most recognizable landmarks in the city. Take some time to admire the Gate and take pictures before heading to the nearby Reichstag Building. The Reichstag is the German parliament building and offers fantastic views of the city from its glass dome. Make sure to book your visit in advance to avoid waiting in long lines.

Next, head to the Berlin Wall Memorial, located just a few minutes away from the Reichstag. This open-air museum provides a moving tribute to the Wall, its victims, and its impact on the city.

Lunch: For lunch, head to the trendy neighborhood of Kreuzberg, which is known for its diverse food scene. There are plenty of options here for every taste and budget, including street food, cafes, and restaurants.

Afternoon: In the afternoon, head to Museum Island, located in the heart of the city. This UNESCO World Heritage Site is home to some of the most important museums and collections in the world. Choose one or two museums to explore, depending on your interests and time available. Some popular options include the Pergamon Museum, the Alte Nationalgalerie, and the Neues Museum.

Evening: As the day winds down, head to the East Side Gallery, which is located along a section of the Berlin Wall that has been preserved as an outdoor gallery. This open-air art exhibition features murals and graffiti by artists from all over the world.

For dinner, head to the trendy neighborhood of Friedrichshain, which is known for its vibrant nightlife and food scene. There are plenty of options here for every taste and budget, including restaurants, bars, and clubs.

End your day by taking a stroll along the Spree River, which runs through the heart of the city. This is a great way to see some of the city's landmarks lit up at night, including the Berlin Cathedral and the TV Tower.

Two-Day Itinerary: Historic Berlin and Trendy Neighborhoods

Day One:

Morning: Start your day at the iconic Berlin Wall Memorial, located just a few minutes away from the Reichstag. This open-air museum provides a moving tribute to the Wall, its victims, and its impact on the city. From here, head to Checkpoint Charlie, one of the most famous crossing points between East and West Berlin during the Cold War. The site now includes a museum that offers a fascinating look at life in divided Berlin.

Next, head to the Jewish Museum Berlin, which explores the history and culture of Germany's Jewish population. The museum's striking architecture is a highlight in itself, and the exhibits offer a powerful reflection on the country's complex and often tragic history.

Lunch: For lunch, head to the trendy neighborhood of Prenzlauer Berg, which is known for its cafes, restaurants, and boutique shops. The Kollwitzplatz area is a great spot to grab a bite to eat and soak up the local atmosphere.

Afternoon: In the afternoon, take a walk through the historic streets of the Nikolaiviertel, the oldest neighborhood in Berlin. This area is full of charming cobblestone streets, historic buildings, and traditional cafes and restaurants.

Evening: For dinner, head to the trendy neighborhood of Neukölln, which is known for its multicultural food scene. There are plenty of options here for every taste and budget, including Turkish, Middle Eastern, and Mediterranean cuisine.

After dinner, head to the historic district of Mitte, which is home to some of Berlin's most famous landmarks, including the Brandenburg Gate and the Berlin Cathedral. Take a stroll through the streets and soak up the historic atmosphere of the city.

Day Two:

Morning: Begin your day by exploring the vibrant neighborhood of Kreuzberg, which is known for its street art, graffiti, and alternative culture. Take a walk through the streets and alleys to discover the neighborhood's unique character.

Next, head to the Berlinische Galerie, a museum of modern art, photography, and architecture. The museum's collection includes works by both international and local artists, and is a great way to experience Berlin's contemporary art scene.

Lunch: For lunch, head to the trendy neighborhood of Friedrichshain, which is known for its food scene and nightlife. There are plenty of options here for every taste and budget, including street food, cafes, and restaurants.

Afternoon: In the afternoon, head to the East Side Gallery, which is located along a section of the Berlin Wall that has been preserved as an outdoor gallery. This open-air art exhibition features murals and graffiti by artists from all over the world.

Evening: For dinner, head to the trendy neighborhood of Charlottenburg-Wilmersdorf, which is known for its upscale dining and shopping. There are plenty of options here for every taste and budget, including high-end restaurants and boutique shops.

End your day by taking a stroll through the historic streets of the neighborhood and soaking up the local atmosphere.

Useful websites:

- Berlin Wall Memorial: https://www.berliner-mauer-gedenkstaette.de/en/

- Checkpoint Charlie: https://www.mauermuseum.de/en

- Jewish Museum Berlin: https://www.jmberlin.de/en

- Prenzlauer Berg: https://www.visitberlin.de/en/prenzlauer-berg

- Nikolaiviertel: https://www.visitberlin.de/en/nikolaiviertel

- Neukölln: https://www.visitberlin.de/en/neukolln

- Kreuzberg: https://www.visitberlin.de/en/kreuzberg

- Berlinische Galerie: https://www.berlinischegalerie.de/en/

- East Side Gallery: https://www.visitberlin.de/en/east-side-gallery

- Friedrichshain: https://www.visitberlin.de/en/friedrichshain

- Charlottenburg-Wilmersdorf: https://www.visitberlin.de/en/charlottenburg-wilmersdorf

Four-Day Itinerary: Day Trips from Berlin

Day One: Potsdam

Take a day trip to Potsdam, the former residence of the Prussian kings and a UNESCO World Heritage Site. Explore the magnificent gardens and palaces of Sanssouci Park, including the stunning Sanssouci Palace and the impressive Neues Palais. Don't miss the chance to stroll through the charming Dutch Quarter and the historic Old Town of Potsdam.

Day Two: Dresden

Visit the historic city of Dresden, which is known for its stunning Baroque architecture and world-class museums. Highlights of the city include the Zwinger Palace, the Frauenkirche, and the Dresden State Art Collections. Take a walk along the Elbe River and enjoy the picturesque views of the city.

Day Three: Hamburg

Take a day trip to Hamburg, one of Germany's most vibrant and exciting cities. Explore the historic harbor area, which is home to the famous Elbphilharmonie concert hall and the bustling Fish Market. Visit the stunning St. Michaelis Church and take a stroll through the trendy neighborhoods of St. Pauli and Sternschanze.

Day Four: Leipzig

Discover the vibrant city of Leipzig, which is known for its rich history, culture, and music scene. Visit the famous St. Thomas Church, where Johann Sebastian Bach once worked as a choir master, and the historic Leipzig Market Square. Don't miss the chance to explore the trendy neighborhoods of Plagwitz and Connewitz, which are full of independent shops, cafes, and restaurants.

Five-Day Itinerary: Berlin and Beyond

Day One: Historic Berlin

Explore the historic heart of Berlin, including the Brandenburg Gate, the Reichstag Building, and the Berlin Wall Memorial. Visit the Jewish Museum Berlin and take a walk through the charming streets of the Nikolaiviertel. In the evening, head to the trendy neighborhood of Neukölln for dinner and drinks.

Day Two: Museum Island and Kreuzberg

Visit Museum Island, home to some of the world's most important museums and collections, including the Pergamon Museum and the Alte Nationalgalerie. In the afternoon, head to the vibrant neighborhood of Kreuzberg, known for its street art, graffiti, and alternative culture.

Day Three: Potsdam

Take a day trip to Potsdam, the former residence of the Prussian kings and a UNESCO World Heritage Site. Explore the magnificent gardens and palaces of Sanssouci Park, including the stunning Sanssouci Palace and the impressive Neues Palais. Don't miss the chance to stroll through the charming Dutch Quarter and the historic Old Town of Potsdam.

Day Four: Dresden

Visit the historic city of Dresden, which is known for its stunning Baroque architecture and world-class museums. Highlights of the city include the Zwinger Palace, the Frauenkirche, and the Dresden State Art Collections. Take a walk along the Elbe River and enjoy the picturesque views of the city.

Day Five: Hamburg

Take a day trip to Hamburg, one of Germany's most vibrant and exciting cities. Explore the historic harbor area, which is home to the famous Elbphilharmonie concert hall and the bustling

Fish Market. Visit the stunning St. Michaelis Church and take a stroll through the trendy neighborhoods of St. Pauli and Sternschanze.

Practical Information for Visiting Berlin

Visa and travel requirements

For most visitors, a visa is not required for travel to Berlin, as Germany is a member of the Schengen Area. However, visitors from some countries may need to obtain a visa before traveling to Berlin. It is recommended that visitors check with their local embassy or consulate to determine if a visa is required.

In addition to a valid passport or ID card, visitors to Berlin should also ensure that they have any necessary travel documents, such as airline tickets or train reservations. It is also a good idea to purchase travel insurance before departing, as this can help protect against unforeseen circumstances such as flight cancellations or medical emergencies.

When traveling to Berlin, visitors should also be aware of any health and safety precautions that may be necessary. It is recommended that visitors check with their healthcare provider to ensure that they are up-to-date on any necessary vaccinations, and that they take necessary precautions to avoid illnesses such as COVID-19. Visitors should also be aware of any safety concerns in the areas they plan to visit, and take necessary precautions such as avoiding dangerous neighborhoods or traveling with a group.

Finally, visitors to Berlin should also be aware of any local customs or laws that may apply. For example, it is considered impolite to tip in Germany, and smoking is prohibited in many public places. Visitors should also be aware that German law requires all visitors to carry a valid form of identification at all times, and that drinking alcohol in public is generally prohibited.

Useful websites:

- https://www.auswaertiges-amt.de/en/einreiseundaufenthalt/visabestimmungen-node

- https://www.germany.travel/en/coronavirus/coronavirus.html

- https://www.who.int/ith/ITH_Annex_I.pdf

- https://www.german-way.com/travel-and-tourism/tipping-in-germany/

- https://www.german-way.com/travel-and-tourism/german-customs-and-culture/

Currency and payment options

The currency used in Berlin and throughout Germany is the Euro (EUR). Visitors can exchange currency at banks, exchange offices, or ATMs, which are widely available throughout the city.

Credit cards are widely accepted in Berlin, and visitors can use Visa, MasterCard, and American Express at most restaurants, hotels, and shops. However, it is a good idea to carry some cash for smaller purchases, as some establishments may not accept credit cards for purchases under a certain amount.

Travelers' checks are not widely accepted in Berlin, and it is generally easier to use a credit card or withdraw cash from an ATM. Visitors should also be aware that many ATMs in Berlin charge a fee for withdrawals, so it is a good idea to check with your bank before traveling to avoid any unexpected charges.

Finally, visitors to Berlin should be aware of any potential currency exchange scams, such as those that offer extremely favorable exchange rates or those that require payment upfront. It is recommended that visitors exchange currency at reputable banks or exchange offices, and avoid exchanging money with strangers on the street.

Useful websites:

- https://www.visitberlin.de/en/practical-information-about-berlin

- https://www.numbeo.com/cost-of-living/in/Berlin

- https://www.tripadvisor.com/Travel-g187323-s601/Berlin:Germany:Money.And.Costs.html

Language and communication tips

The official language of Berlin and throughout Germany is German, but English is widely spoken, especially in tourist areas. Visitors should have no problem communicating in English, as many signs and menus are often available in both German and English.

However, it is always appreciated when visitors make an effort to speak some basic German phrases, such as "hello" (hallo), "please" (bitte), and "thank you" (danke). Learning a few key phrases can help visitors feel more comfortable and make it easier to navigate the city and interact with locals.

Visitors to Berlin should also be aware that Germans tend to be more reserved than people in some other countries, and may not always initiate conversation with strangers. However, this should not be interpreted as unfriendliness, and visitors should not hesitate to ask for help or directions if needed.

Finally, visitors to Berlin should be aware of any cultural differences that may affect communication. For example, Germans tend to be more direct and less likely to use small talk or pleasantries in conversation. Visitors should also be aware that punctuality is highly valued in German culture, and it is considered impolite to be late for appointments or meetings.

Useful websites:

- https://www.visitberlin.de/en/plan/basic-information

- https://www.tripsavvy.com/german-language-tips-for-travelers-4065846

- https://www.internations.org/go/moving-to-germany/language-communication

Events and Festivals:

Berlin is home to a wide variety of events and festivals throughout the year, ranging from music and cultural festivals to seasonal celebrations and sporting events. Visitors to Berlin can find something to suit their interests and schedule, no matter when they visit.

One of the most popular events in Berlin is the Berlin International Film Festival, also known as the Berlinale, which takes place every February. This festival attracts filmmakers, industry professionals, and film lovers from around the world, and features screenings, workshops, and other events.

Another popular event in Berlin is the Berlin Marathon, which takes place every September and is one of the largest marathons in the world. This event attracts runners and spectators from around the world, and features a scenic course through the city's streets.

Other popular events and festivals in Berlin include the Carnival of Cultures in May, the Berlin Music Week in September, and the Berlin Art Week in September. There are also many seasonal celebrations throughout the year, such as the Christmas markets in December and the New Year's Eve celebrations at the Brandenburg Gate.

Visitors to Berlin can find information on upcoming events and festivals by checking local event calendars, such as VisitBerlin or Berlin.de, or by visiting the local tourist information center. Some events may require tickets or advanced reservations, so visitors should plan accordingly.

Useful websites:

- https://www.visitberlin.de/en/events-calendar

- https://www.berlin.de/en/events/

- https://www.berlin.de/en/tourism/plan/events/

- https://www.berlinale.de/en/home.html

- https://www.bmw-berlin-marathon.com/en/

Health and safety information

Berlin is generally a safe city for visitors, with a low crime rate and a well-developed infrastructure. However, visitors should take necessary precautions to ensure their safety and well-being.

One potential concern for visitors is the risk of pickpocketing or theft, especially in crowded tourist areas or on public transportation. Visitors should be aware of their surroundings and take necessary precautions, such as keeping their valuables secure and avoiding carrying large amounts of cash.

Visitors to Berlin should also be aware of any potential health risks, such as exposure to pollution or illnesses. It is recommended that visitors check with their healthcare provider to ensure that they are up-to-date on any necessary vaccinations, and that they take necessary precautions to avoid illnesses such as COVID-19. Visitors should also be aware of any potential air pollution or water contamination, and take necessary precautions such as wearing a mask or avoiding swimming in certain areas.

Finally, visitors to Berlin should be aware of any local laws and customs that may affect their safety. For example, drinking alcohol in public is generally prohibited, and visitors should be aware of any areas that may be dangerous, especially at night. Visitors should also be aware that German law requires all visitors to carry a valid form of identification at all times.

Emergency Numbers

In case of an emergency in Berlin, visitors should call the appropriate emergency number to receive assistance from the police, fire department, or medical services. It is important to have these numbers readily available in case of an emergency.

The emergency number for all services in Germany is 112. This number can be used to contact police, fire department, and medical services in case of an emergency.

For non-emergency police assistance, visitors can also call the police hotline at 110. This number can be used to report crimes or other incidents that do not require immediate emergency assistance.

Visitors to Berlin should also be aware of any additional emergency numbers that may be specific to their country of origin. For example, visitors from the United States can contact the U.S. Embassy in Berlin in case of an emergency by calling +49 (0) 30 8305 0.

It is recommended that visitors program these emergency numbers into their mobile phones or keep them in a safe and accessible location in case of an emergency.

Key Embassies

Berlin is home to a number of foreign embassies and consulates, providing assistance and support for citizens of those countries. Visitors to Berlin should be aware of the location and contact details of their embassy in case of an emergency or other need for assistance.

Here are some of the key embassies and their contact details in Berlin:

1. United States Embassy: Address: Pariser Platz 2, 10117 Berlin Phone: +49 30 83050 Website: https://de.usembassy.gov/

2. British Embassy: Address: Wilhelmstraße 70-71, 10117 Berlin Phone: +49 30 204570 Website: https://www.gov.uk/world/organisations/british-embassy-berlin

3. French Embassy: Address: Pariser Platz 5, 10117 Berlin Phone: +49 30 59003 9100 Website: https://de.ambafrance.org/

4. Canadian Embassy: Address: Leipziger Platz 17, 10117 Berlin Phone: +49 30 203120 Website: https://www.canadainternational.gc.ca/germany-allemagne/

5. Australian Embassy: Address: Wallstraße 76-79, 10179 Berlin Phone: +49 30 8800880 Website: https://germany.embassy.gov.au/

Visitors should note that embassy hours and availability may vary, and it is recommended to check the embassy website or contact them directly for more information.

Useful Phrases in German

Greetings:

- Hallo (Hello)
- Guten Morgen (Good morning)
- Guten Tag (Good day)
- Guten Abend (Good evening)
- Tschüss (Bye)

Basic Phrases:

- Ja (Yes)
- Nein (No)
- Bitte (Please)
- Danke (Thank you)
- Entschuldigung (Excuse me)
- Es tut mir leid (I'm sorry)
- Wie geht es Ihnen? (How are you?)
- Mir geht es gut, danke. (I'm fine, thank you.)
- Sprechen Sie Englisch? (Do you speak English?)
- Ich spreche kein Deutsch. (I don't speak German.)
- Können Sie mir helfen? (Can you help me?)
- Wo ist...? (Where is...?)
- Wie viel kostet das? (How much does that cost?)
- Ich möchte... (I would like...)
- Ich verstehe nicht. (I don't understand.)
- Ich habe mich verlaufen. (I'm lost.)

Food and Drink:

- Ich möchte einen Kaffee, bitte. (I would like a coffee, please.)
- Eine Tasse Tee, bitte. (A cup of tea, please.)
- Ich hätte gerne ein Bier. (I would like a beer.)
- Ich möchte etwas zu essen bestellen. (I would like to order some food.)
- Die Rechnung, bitte. (The bill, please.)

Transportation:

- Wo ist der Bahnhof? (Where is the train station?)
- Wo kann ich eine Fahrkarte kaufen? (Where can I buy a ticket?)
- Ich möchte eine Fahrkarte nach... (I would like a ticket to...)
- Wann fährt der nächste Zug? (When does the next train leave?)
- Wo ist die U-Bahn-Station? (Where is the subway station?)

- Wie komme ich zum Flughafen? (How do I get to the airport?)

Numbers:

- Eins (One)
- Zwei (Two)
- Drei (Three)
- Vier (Four)
- Fünf (Five)
- Sechs (Six)
- Sieben (Seven)
- Acht (Eight)
- Neun (Nine)
- Zehn (Ten)

Remember, learning a few basic phrases in the local language can make a big difference in your travel experience, so don't be afraid to practice and use them!

Thank You!

Berlin is a vibrant and exciting city, full of history, culture, and attractions for visitors to explore. From the historic landmarks of the Brandenburg Gate and the Berlin Wall, to the world-class museums and trendy neighborhoods, there is something for everyone in this dynamic city.

Visitors to Berlin can also take advantage of the city's excellent food and drink scene, with traditional cuisine and craft beer, as well as trendy cafes and cocktail bars.

With its central location in Europe, Berlin also makes an excellent base for day trips to nearby cities such as Potsdam, Dresden, Hamburg, and Leipzig.

Whether you're visiting for a weekend or a longer stay, Berlin is sure to leave a lasting impression. We hope that this travel guide has provided you with the information and inspiration you need to plan your trip and make the most of your time in this amazing city.

Have a fantastic time in Berlin!

Your friends at Guidora.

Copyright Notice

Guidora Berlin in 3 Days Travel Guide ©

Disclaimer

The publishers have checked the information in this travel guide, but its accuracy is not warranted or guaranteed. Berlin visitors are advised that opening times should always be checked before making a journey.

Tracing Copyright Owners

Every effort has been made to trace the copyright holders of referred material. Where these efforts have not been successful, copyright owners are invited to contact the Editor (Guidora) so that their copyright can be acknowledged and/or the material removed from the publication.

Creative Commons Content

We are most grateful to publishers of Creative Commons material, including images. Our policies concerning this material are (1) to credit the copyright owner, and provide a link where possible (2) to remove Creative Commons material, at once, if the copyright owner so requests - for example, if the owner changes the licensing of an image.

We will also keep our interpretation of the Creative Commons Non-Commercial license under review. Along with, we believe, most web publishers, our current view is that acceptance of the 'Non-

Commercial' condition means (1) we must not sell the image or any publication containing the image (2) we may, however, use an image as an illustration for some information which is not being sold or offered for sale.

Note to other copyright owners

We are grateful to those copyright owners who have given permission for their material to be used. Some of the material comes from secondary and tertiary sources. In every case, we have tried to locate the original author or photographer and make the appropriate acknowledgment. In some cases, the sources have proved obscure and we have been unable to track them down. In these cases, we would like to hear from the copyright owners and will be pleased to acknowledge them in future editions or remove the material.

Printed in Great Britain
by Amazon

46370511R00056